Broomstick Lace Crochet

Timeless Techniques and Modern Projects

Diana Dennis

copyright@2024

Table of Content

CHAPTER ONE
The Unveiling

What is Broomstick Lace Crochet?

Broomstick Lace Crochet is a distinctive crochet technique characterized by its lacy, openwork pattern. It's named for the tool traditionally used to create the stitches, which was a broomstick handle.

Technique: Broomstick Lace involves using a large crochet hook or a broomstick handle to create loops of yarn, which are then worked into a lacy pattern using a smaller crochet hook.

Stitches: The basic stitch involves pulling up loops of yarn over the broomstick, then working those loops into a pattern using a crochet hook.

Broomstick Lace is valued for its intricate appearance and the beautiful, light, and airy fabric it creates.

Brief History and Origin

Broomstick Lace Crochet has a history rooted in traditional crochet techniques. The name "broomstick lace" comes from the original use of a broomstick handle as a tool to create the large loops characteristic of the stitch. This technique was popularized in the early 20th century but draws from older lace-making traditions.

The method involves creating loops of yarn over a large cylindrical object and then working them with a smaller crochet hook to form a lacy pattern. It was a practical solution for creating intricate lace patterns with minimal tools. Over time, the technique evolved and became known for its distinctive and elegant lacework.

Tools and Materials Needed

To get started with Broomstick Lace Crochet, you'll need the following tools and materials:

Yarn: Choose a yarn with a smooth texture to highlight the lace pattern. Lighter weight yarns like DK or worsted are commonly used, but you can experiment with different types.

Crochet Hooks:

Large Hook: For creating the loops on the broomstick. This is often larger than the hook used for the main crochet work.

Smaller Hook: For working the loops into the final pattern. The size will depend on your yarn and pattern requirements.

Broomstick Handle or Alternative Tool: A large cylindrical object like a broomstick handle, knitting needle, or a specialized broomstick lace tool can be used to form the loops.

Scissors: For cutting yarn ends.

Yarn Needle: For weaving in ends and finishing off your project.

How to Hold the Broomstick

To hold the broomstick (or equivalent tool) correctly for Broomstick Lace Crochet:

Position the Tool: Hold the broomstick handle or large cylindrical object horizontally or vertically in front of you, depending on your comfort and the pattern you're using.

Grip: Use your dominant hand to hold the broomstick securely. Your fingers should be positioned comfortably around the tool, with your thumb and index finger acting as the primary grip. The other fingers can rest lightly on the tool for additional support.

Placement: Ensure that the broomstick is positioned so that the yarn can easily be wrapped around it without too much tension. The tool should be parallel to your work surface for easy maneuverability.

Stabilization: If needed, use your non-dominant hand to stabilize the yarn and help guide it as you wrap it around the broomstick. This can help keep the loops even and consistent.

CHAPTER TWO
Broomstick Lace Crochet Techniques

Basic Techniques

Creating the Foundation Chain

Make a Slip Knot: Start by making a slip knot on your crochet hook. This knot will be your first stitch.

Chain Stitches: Yarn over and pull through the slip knot to make a chain stitch. Repeat this process to create the required number of chain stitches for your project. The foundation chain forms the base of your Broomstick Lace pattern.

Check Length: Ensure that the foundation chain is the desired length according to your pattern. It should be loose and not too tight.

Working the Basic Broomstick Lace Stitch

Wrap Yarn Around the Broomstick: Insert the large hook or broomstick handle into the first chain stitch. Yarn over and pull up a loop, which will be placed on the broomstick. Continue pulling up loops across the foundation chain, placing each loop onto the broomstick.

Prepare to Work the Loops: Once you have all the loops on the broomstick, remove the broomstick carefully. Hold the loops in place with your fingers to prevent them from sliding off.

Work the Loops: Insert your smaller crochet hook into the first loop on the broomstick. Yarn over and pull through both the loop and the stitch to create a single crochet. Repeat this process for each loop, working them into the final pattern according to your design.

Complete the Row: Once all the loops are worked, you'll have a row of Broomstick Lace stitches. Follow the pattern to continue with additional rows or patterns as required.

Single Broomstick Lace Stitch

Create Foundation Chain: Start with a foundation chain of the desired length.

Wrap Yarn: Insert the large hook or broomstick into the first chain stitch. Yarn over and pull up a loop, placing it onto the broomstick. Continue pulling up loops across the entire row.

Remove Broomstick: After placing all the loops on the broomstick, carefully remove the broomstick while holding the loops in place.

Insert Smaller Hook: Insert the smaller crochet hook through the first loop on the broomstick. Yarn over and pull through both the loop and the stitch on the hook, completing a single crochet. Repeat this process for each loop.

Finish the Row: Continue working each loop with single crochet stitches until you reach the end of the row.

Double Broomstick Lace Stitch

Create Foundation Chain: Start with a foundation chain of the required length.

Wrap Yarn: Insert the large hook or broomstick into the first chain stitch. Yarn over and pull up a loop, placing it onto the broomstick. Continue pulling up loops across the foundation chain.

Remove Broomstick: Once all loops are on the broomstick, carefully remove it while holding the loops in place.

Work Double Crochet: Insert your smaller crochet hook into the first loop on the broomstick. Yarn over, pull through the loop, yarn over again, pull through the first two loops on the hook, yarn over once more, and pull through the remaining two loops. This completes a double crochet. Repeat for each loop.

Complete the Row: Continue working each loop into a double crochet stitch to complete the row.

Advanced Techniques

Incorporating Color Changes

Complete a Row: Finish a row of Broomstick Lace with your current color.

Prepare for Color Change: At the end of the row, do not finish the last stitch with the current color. Instead, complete the stitch until there are two loops left on your hook.

Introduce New Color: Yarn over with the new color and pull through the two remaining loops on your hook to complete the stitch. This changes the color of your project.

Work with New Color: Continue with the new color for the next rows as required by your pattern. Follow the pattern's instructions for where and how to incorporate color changes.

Secure and Weave Ends: After finishing your project, weave in any loose ends from the color changes using a yarn needle.

Adding Edges and Borders

Complete Your Main Project: Finish the main body of your Broomstick Lace project according to your pattern.

Choose an Edge or Border Pattern: Select a border pattern that complements your project. Common choices include single crochet, double crochet, or decorative lace borders.

Attach Yarn: At the end of the last row of your main project, attach your border yarn by making a slipknot and joining it to the edge.

Work the Border:

Single Crochet Border: Insert the hook into the edge of the project, yarn over, pull through, yarn over again, and pull through both loops on the hook. Continue working single crochet stitches evenly along the edge.

Double Crochet Border: Yarn over, insert the hook into the edge of the project, yarn over, pull through, yarn over again, pull through the first two loops on the hook, yarn over, and pull through the remaining two loops. Continue evenly along the edge.

Lace Border: Follow your chosen lace border pattern, which may involve working chain spaces and additional stitches.

Finish the Border: Complete the border according to your pattern. Fasten off the yarn and weave in any loose ends with a yarn needle.

Working with Different Yarn Types

Choose Yarn: Select a different yarn type that complements or contrasts with your main yarn. For example, you might use a variegated yarn or a different texture, such as a fluffy or metallic yarn.

Test Swatch: Before starting your project, create a small swatch with the new yarn to ensure that it works well with your chosen pattern and hook sizes. This helps you see how the yarn affects the final look.

Start Project: Begin your project with the new yarn type. Follow the basic Broomstick Lace techniques but be mindful of any changes in texture or drape due to the different yarn.

Adjust Tension and Hook Size: Depending on the yarn type, you might need to adjust your tension or use a different hook size to accommodate the yarn's characteristics.

Complete and Finish: Finish your project as usual. If the new yarn has a different texture, consider how it will affect the final appearance and handle accordingly.

Creating Textured Patterns

Select a Textured Pattern: Choose a pattern that incorporates textures such as puff stitches, bobbles, or ribbing along with Broomstick Lace. Textured patterns add visual interest and complexity.

Work Broomstick Lace Base: Start by creating a foundation chain and working the Broomstick Lace stitches as usual to establish the base of your textured pattern.

Incorporate Texture:

Puff Stitches: Yarn over and insert your hook into the stitch or space, yarn over and pull up a loop, yarn over and pull through the loops on the hook to complete the puff stitch. Repeat as needed according to the pattern.

Bobble Stitches: Yarn over, insert the hook into the stitch or space, yarn over and pull up a loop, yarn over and pull through the first two loops, yarn over again and pull through the remaining loops on the hook to complete the bobble.

Combine Techniques: Integrate the textured stitches with the Broomstick Lace by alternating between the two techniques or working the textured stitches in specific areas to highlight them.

Complete and Finish: Follow the pattern to finish the project, ensuring that the textured areas are even and well-integrated with the Broomstick Lace sections. Weave in any ends and block the project if necessary to enhance the texture.

Adding Embellishments

Adding embellishments to Broomstick Lace Crochet projects can enhance their beauty and uniqueness.

Adding Beads

Choose Beads: Select beads that complement your yarn. Beads with large enough holes to fit over your yarn or stitches are ideal.

Prepare Beads: Pre-thread the beads onto your yarn if you want them evenly spaced. For this, cut a length of yarn, thread the beads onto it, and then use this yarn as you crochet.

Crochet with Beads: As you work your Broomstick Lace, insert a bead by placing it on the hook before pulling through the yarn. Beads can be added to specific stitches or evenly throughout the project.

Secure Beads: Ensure that beads are properly placed and do not disrupt the flow of your stitches. You can also use a needle to move the beads to the desired position.

Adding Appliqué or Embroidery

Select Embellishments: Choose appliqué shapes or embroidery designs that complement your Broomstick Lace project. These could be flowers, stars, or other motifs.

Position Appliqué: Place the appliqué on your project where you want it to be attached. Use fabric glue or a temporary stitch to secure it in place before permanently attaching it.

Attach Appliqué:

Sewing: Using a yarn needle and matching yarn or thread, sew the appliqué onto your project with small, neat stitches.

Crocheting: If the appliqué is crochet-based, you can attach it by crocheting it directly onto the project in the desired location.

Add Embroidery: For embroidery, use a yarn needle and embroidery floss or thread to stitch designs over your Broomstick Lace. This can include simple patterns or more intricate designs.

Secure and Finish: Ensure all embellishments are securely attached and weave in any loose ends to finish.

CHAPTER THREE
Beginner Projects

Broomstick Lace Scarf

Materials:

- Yarn: DK or worsted weight yarn
- Hook: Large hook for loops (e.g., 6.0 mm or larger) and smaller hook for working stitches (e.g., 4.0 mm)
- Broomstick handle or large knitting needle

Instructions:

Create Foundation Chain: Chain 20 to 30 stitches, or the length desired for your scarf.

Work Loops: Using the large hook or broomstick, pull up loops across the foundation chain and place them onto the broomstick.

Work the Stitches: Remove the broomstick and use the smaller hook to work each loop into a single crochet or double crochet, depending on the pattern.

Continue Rows: Repeat the process for additional rows until your scarf reaches the desired length.

Finish Edges: Add a simple border if desired, such as single crochet or double crochet stitches around the edges. Weave in any loose ends.

Result: A light, lacy scarf that's perfect for practicing the basic Broomstick Lace techniques.

Broomstick Lace Bookmark

Materials:

- Yarn: Lightweight yarn or thread
- Hook: Large hook for loops (e.g., 4.0 mm) and smaller hook for working stitches (e.g., 2.5 mm)
- Broomstick handle or large knitting needle

Instructions:

Create Foundation Chain: Chain 10 to 15 stitches, depending on the width you want for your bookmark.

Work Loops: Using the large hook or broomstick, pull up loops across the foundation chain and place them onto the broomstick.

Work the Stitches: Remove the broomstick and use the smaller hook to work each loop into a single crochet or double crochet.

Add a Fringe (Optional): After finishing the body of the bookmark, you can add a fringe to the bottom for extra decoration. Cut several pieces of yarn, fold them in half, and attach them to the end of the bookmark with a simple knot.

Finish: Weave in any loose ends. Block the bookmark if necessary to shape it.

Result: A practical and elegant bookmark that showcases the delicate beauty of Broomstick Lace while being a quick and simple project.

Broomstick Lace Coaster

Materials:

- Yarn: Cotton or acrylic yarn (medium weight)
- Hook: Large hook for loops (e.g., 5.0 mm or 6.0 mm) and smaller hook for working stitches (e.g., 4.0 mm)
- Broomstick handle or large knitting needle

Instructions:

Create Foundation Chain: Chain 10 to 12 stitches to form a small circle.

Work Loops: Using the large hook or broomstick, pull up loops across the foundation chain and place them onto the broomstick.

Work the Stitches: Remove the broomstick and use the smaller hook to work each loop into a single crochet or double crochet.

Add Rounds (Optional): For a larger coaster, you can add additional rounds of Broomstick Lace or regular crochet stitches.

Finish Edges: Add a simple border if desired, such as a round of single crochet or slip stitches around the edge. Weave in any loose ends.

Result: A stylish and functional coaster that showcases the Broomstick Lace technique and can protect surfaces from hot or cold beverages.

Broomstick Lace Headband

Materials:

- Yarn: Worsted weight yarn
- Hook: Large hook for loops (e.g., 6.0 mm) and smaller hook for working stitches (e.g., 5.0 mm)
- Broomstick handle or large knitting needle

Instructions:

Create Foundation Chain: Chain 10 to 15 stitches, adjusting based on the size needed for the headband.

Work Loops: Using the large hook or broomstick, pull up loops across the foundation chain and place them onto the broomstick.

Work the Stitches: Remove the broomstick and use the smaller hook to work each loop into a single crochet or double crochet.

Continue Rows: Repeat the process to reach the desired width of the headband. The length should be enough to fit around your head comfortably.

Join Ends: Once the headband is the right length, join the ends together by sewing or crocheting them together to form a loop.

Finish: Weave in any loose ends and block the headband if needed.

Result: A fashionable and cozy headband that demonstrates the beauty of Broomstick Lace and provides a practical accessory for cool weather.

Broomstick Lace Dishcloth

Materials:

- Yarn: Cotton yarn (medium weight, such as worsted weight)
- Hook: Large hook for loops (e.g., 5.0 mm or 6.0 mm) and smaller hook for working stitches (e.g., 4.0 mm or 5.0 mm)
- Broomstick handle or large knitting needle

Instructions:

Create Foundation Chain: Chain 30 to 40 stitches, depending on the size of the dishcloth you want.

Work Loops: Using the large hook or broomstick, pull up loops across the foundation chain and place them onto the broomstick.

Work the Stitches: Remove the broomstick and use the smaller hook to work each loop into a single crochet or double crochet.

Continue Rows: Repeat the process for additional rows until the dishcloth reaches the desired size.

Finish Edges: Add a simple border if desired, such as single crochet or slip stitches around the edges. Weave in any loose ends.

Result: A practical and absorbent dishcloth that highlights the airy texture of Broomstick Lace while being useful in the kitchen.

Broomstick Lace Baby Blanket

Materials:

- Yarn: Soft baby yarn or acrylic yarn (medium to bulky weight)
- Hook: Large hook for loops (e.g., 6.0 mm or 7.0 mm) and smaller hook for working stitches (e.g., 5.0 mm or 6.0 mm)
- Broomstick handle or large knitting needle

Instructions:

Create Foundation Chain: Chain 60 to 80 stitches, depending on the desired width of the blanket.

Work Loops: Using the large hook or broomstick, pull up loops across the foundation chain and place them onto the broomstick.

Work the Stitches: Remove the broomstick and use the smaller hook to work each loop into a single crochet or double crochet.

Continue Rows: Repeat the process for additional rows until the blanket reaches the desired length.

Add Border: Optionally, add a border around the blanket using single crochet, double crochet, or a decorative edging. Weave in any loose ends.

Result: A soft and cozy baby blanket that combines the beauty of Broomstick Lace with a practical, comforting design.

CHAPTER FOUR
Intermediate Projects

Broomstick Lace Shawl

Materials:

- Yarn: Lightweight or DK weight yarn (preferably with some drape)
- Hook: Large hook for loops (e.g., 6.0 mm) and smaller hook for working stitches (e.g., 5.0 mm)
- Broomstick handle or large knitting needle

Instructions:

Create Foundation Chain: Chain 80 to 100 stitches, or the desired width of your shawl.

Work Loops: Using the large hook or broomstick, pull up loops across the foundation chain and place them onto the broomstick.

Work the Stitches: Remove the broomstick and use the smaller hook to work each loop into a single crochet or double crochet.

Shape the Shawl:

Increase: To shape the shawl, add increases by working extra stitches at the beginning and end of each row.

Add Pattern: Incorporate a pattern by alternating between Broomstick Lace and another stitch pattern, such as clusters or shells.

Continue Rows: Work additional rows, following the pattern for increases and stitch variations.

Finish Edges: Add a decorative border, such as a scalloped edge or a row of picot stitches. Weave in any loose ends.

Result: A stylish and versatile shawl that highlights the Broomstick Lace technique while incorporating shaping and pattern variations.

Broomstick Lace Poncho

Materials:

- Yarn: Worsted or bulky weight yarn
- Hook: Large hook for loops (e.g., 6.0 mm or 7.0 mm) and smaller hook for working stitches (e.g., 5.0 mm or 6.0 mm)
- Broomstick handle or large knitting needle

Instructions:

Create Foundation Chain: Chain enough stitches to form the width of the poncho, typically 80 to 120 stitches.

Work Loops: Using the large hook or broomstick, pull up loops across the foundation chain and place them onto the broomstick.

Work the Stitches: Remove the broomstick and use the smaller hook to work each loop into a single crochet or double crochet.

Shape the Poncho:

Front and Back Panels: Work two panels separately, or work in the round if preferred.

Increase and Decrease: Add increases for shaping the top and decreases to shape the sides as you work down.

Join Panels: If working separate panels, sew or crochet the panels together at the sides, leaving openings for the arms.

Add Edges: Finish with a border or edging around the neck and hem of the poncho. Consider a simple scalloped or shell stitch for decoration.

Result: A warm and fashionable poncho that combines the airy beauty of Broomstick Lace with practical wearability and shaping.

Broomstick Lace Vest

Materials:

- Yarn: DK or worsted weight yarn
- Hook: Large hook for loops (e.g., 6.0 mm) and smaller hook for working stitches (e.g., 5.0 mm)
- Broomstick handle or large knitting needle

Instructions:

Create Foundation Chain: Chain enough stitches to match the width of your vest. Typically, this would be about 100 to 150 stitches depending on size.

Work Loops: Pull up loops across the foundation chain and place them onto the broomstick.

Work the Stitches: Remove the broomstick and use the smaller hook to work each loop into a single crochet or double crochet.

Shape the Vest:

Front and Back Panels: Work the front and back panels separately. Increase or decrease stitches as needed to shape the armholes and necklines.

Join Panels: After completing the panels, sew or crochet them together at the shoulders and sides, leaving openings for the arms.

Add Edging: Add a border around the armholes and neckline. Options include simple single crochet, picot edges, or a more decorative pattern.

Finish: Weave in any loose ends and block the vest to shape it properly.

Result: A fashionable and versatile vest that showcases Broomstick Lace with the added complexity of shaping and assembly.

Broomstick Lace Wrap

Materials:

- Yarn: Lightweight or DK weight yarn
- Hook: Large hook for loops (e.g., 6.0 mm) and smaller hook for working stitches (e.g., 5.0 mm)
- Broomstick handle or large knitting needle

Instructions:

Create Foundation Chain: Chain 150 to 200 stitches, or the length needed for your wrap.

Work Loops: Using the large hook or broomstick, pull up loops across the foundation chain and place them onto the broomstick.

Work the Stitches: Remove the broomstick and use the smaller hook to work each loop into a single crochet or double crochet.

Add Pattern: For added interest, incorporate alternating rows of Broomstick Lace and other stitch patterns such as shell stitches or puff stitches.

Continue Rows: Continue working rows in your chosen pattern until the wrap reaches the desired width and length.

Finish Edges: Add a decorative border, such as a scalloped or fringed edge. Weave in any loose ends.

Result: A stylish and cozy wrap that combines the airy texture of Broomstick Lace with versatile patterns and a decorative finish.

CHAPTER FIVE
Advanced Projects

Broomstick Lace Shawl with Lace Edging

Materials:

- Yarn: Lightweight or DK weight yarn (choose a yarn with good drape, such as silk or bamboo)
- Hook: Large hook for loops (e.g., 6.0 mm) and smaller hook for working stitches (e.g., 5.0 mm)
- Broomstick handle or large knitting needle

Instructions:

Create Foundation Chain: Chain enough stitches to form the width of the shawl, typically around 150 to 200 stitches.

Work Loops: Using the large hook or broomstick, pull up loops across the foundation chain and place them onto the broomstick.

Work the Stitches: Remove the broomstick and use the smaller hook to work each loop into a single crochet or double crochet.

Add Pattern: Integrate intricate patterns by alternating rows of Broomstick Lace with stitch patterns such as shells, clusters, or openwork lace.

Shape the Shawl: Incorporate increases at the edges or center to create a triangular or crescent shape, depending on your preference.

Add Lace Edging:

Work Edge: Create a lace border by working a delicate lace pattern around the edges of the shawl. Popular choices include scallops, picots, or lace motifs.

Attach Border: Attach the lace border to the shawl, ensuring a smooth transition from the main body to the edging.

Finish: Weave in any loose ends and block the shawl to enhance the lace patterns and shape.

Result: A sophisticated and elegant shawl that combines the airy beauty of Broomstick Lace with detailed lace edging for a high-impact, fashion-forward accessory.

Broomstick Lace Throw Blanket with Colorwork

Materials:

- Yarn: Medium or bulky weight yarn in multiple colors
- Hook: Large hook for loops (e.g., 7.0 mm) and smaller hook for working stitches (e.g., 6.0 mm)
- Broomstick handle or large knitting needle

Instructions:

Create Foundation Chain: Chain enough stitches to reach the desired width of the throw blanket, typically around 150 to 200 stitches.

Work Loops: Using the large hook or broomstick, pull up loops across the foundation chain and place them onto the broomstick.

Work the Stitches: Remove the broomstick and use the smaller hook to work each loop into a single crochet or double crochet.

Incorporate Colorwork:

Change Colors: Introduce color changes by switching yarn colors at the beginning or end of a row. Use the new color to pull up loops and work stitches.

Pattern: Create color patterns by alternating between colors, incorporating stripes, blocks, or motifs.

Continue Rows: Work rows with color changes and pattern variations until the blanket reaches the desired length.

Add Edging: Finish with a coordinating border or edge that complements the colorwork. Options include a simple border in one color or a more complex edge that incorporates multiple colors.

Finish: Weave in all loose ends, and block the throw blanket to smooth out any color transitions and shape the blanket properly.

Result: A visually striking throw blanket that showcases advanced Broomstick Lace techniques with colorful patterns and a polished finish.

Broomstick Lace Cardigan

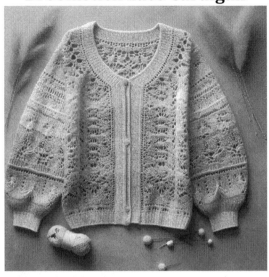

Materials:

- Yarn: Medium or bulky weight yarn
- Hook: Large hook for loops (e.g., 6.0 mm or 7.0 mm) and smaller hook for working stitches (e.g., 5.0 mm or 6.0 mm)
- Broomstick handle or large knitting needle

Instructions:

Create Foundation Chain: Chain enough stitches to match the width of the back panel of the cardigan. This will depend on your size and design.

Work Loops: Using the large hook or broomstick, pull up loops across the foundation chain and place them onto the broomstick.

Work the Stitches: Remove the broomstick and use the smaller hook to work each loop into a single crochet or double crochet.

Shape the Panels:

Back Panel: Continue working rows until the panel reaches the desired length for the back of the cardigan.

Front Panels: Work two separate panels for the front, shaping armholes and necklines as needed.

Sleeves: Create sleeves by working smaller panels or tubes with Broomstick Lace and shaping them to fit.

Assemble Cardigan:

Sew Panels: Attach the back and front panels at the shoulders and sides, leaving openings for the arms.

Attach Sleeves: Sew or crochet the sleeves to the armholes.

Add Edging: Add a border around the neck, front edges, and cuffs. Options include a simple ribbing or a decorative lace edge.

Finish: Weave in any loose ends, and block the cardigan to shape it properly.

Result: A stylish and functional cardigan that combines the elegance of Broomstick Lace with the complexity of garment construction and shaping.

Broomstick Lace Table Runner with Motifs

Materials:

- Yarn: Medium weight or cotton yarn
- Hook: Large hook for loops (e.g., 5.0 mm or 6.0 mm) and smaller hook for

working stitches (e.g., 4.0 mm or 5.0 mm)

- Broomstick handle or large knitting needle

Instructions:

Create Foundation Chain: Chain enough stitches to match the width of your table runner. Typically, this would be about 50 to 70 stitches.

Work Loops: Using the large hook or broomstick, pull up loops across the foundation chain and place them onto the broomstick.

Work the Stitches: Remove the broomstick and use the smaller hook to work each loop into a single crochet or double crochet.

Add Motifs:

Create Motifs: Work individual motifs such as flowers, stars, or geometric shapes using a combination of Broomstick Lace and other crochet techniques.

Attach Motifs: Attach the motifs to the main body of the runner as you work, either by crocheting them directly onto the runner or by sewing them on afterward.

Continue Rows: Work additional rows of Broomstick Lace, incorporating more motifs as desired.

Add Edging: Finish with a decorative border around the entire table runner. Options include scalloped edges, picots, or a simple lace trim.

Finish: Weave in any loose ends and block the table runner to enhance the motifs and shape.

Result: A beautiful and intricate table runner that showcases advanced Broomstick Lace techniques and decorative motifs, adding elegance to any table setting.

Broomstick Lace Poncho with Color Gradients

Materials:

- Yarn: Worsted or bulky weight yarn in multiple colors (for gradient effects)
- Hook: Large hook for loops (e.g., 7.0 mm) and smaller hook for working stitches (e.g., 6.0 mm)
- Broomstick handle or large knitting needle

Instructions:

Create Foundation Chain: Chain enough stitches to match the width of the poncho, typically around 120 to 150 stitches.

Work Loops: Using the large hook or broomstick, pull up loops across the foundation chain and place them onto the broomstick.

Work the Stitches: Remove the broomstick and use the smaller hook to work each loop into a single crochet or double crochet.

Incorporate Color Gradients:

Gradient Transition: Introduce a color gradient by gradually changing yarn colors every few rows. This can create a smooth color transition effect.

Color Blending: Work a few rows with each color, blending them to achieve a gradient effect.

Shape the Poncho: Increase stitches as needed to shape the poncho. For a classic poncho, shape it into a large square or rectangle and join the sides.

Add Edging: Finish with a coordinating border around the neck and hem, such as a scalloped or picot edge.

Finish: Weave in any loose ends and block the poncho to set the shape and enhance the gradient colors.

Result: A striking poncho with a beautiful gradient color effect that combines Broomstick Lace with advanced colorwork.

Broomstick Lace Lace Panel Skirt

Materials:

- Yarn: Lightweight or DK weight yarn
- Hook: Large hook for loops (e.g., 6.0 mm) and smaller hook for working stitches (e.g., 5.0 mm)
- Broomstick handle or large knitting needle
- Elastic waistband or drawstring for the skirt

Instructions:

Create Foundation Chain: Chain enough stitches to match the width of the skirt panel. This will vary based on size and design, typically around 120 to 150 stitches.

Work Loops: Using the large hook or broomstick, pull up loops across the foundation chain and place them onto the broomstick.

Work the Stitches: Remove the broomstick and use the smaller hook to work each loop into a single crochet or double crochet.

Add Lace Panels:

Create Panels: Work additional panels for the skirt, incorporating Broomstick Lace and other lace patterns such as shell stitches or eyelets.

Shape Panels: Incorporate increases or decreases to shape the panels and create a flared effect.

Assemble Skirt: Join the panels together to form a skirt. Attach an elastic waistband or drawstring to the top edge of the skirt for a fitted waist.

Add Edging: Finish with a decorative edge at the hem, such as a lace trim or scalloped border.

Finish: Weave in any loose ends and block the skirt to set the lace patterns and shape.

Result: An elegant and fashionable skirt with intricate Broomstick Lace panels and a custom waistband, perfect for special occasions or as a stylish wardrobe piece.

CHAPTER SIX
Troubleshooting

Loops Too Tight or Too Loose

Issue: If your loops are too tight, they can be difficult to work with. If they are too loose, they may create an uneven texture.

Troubleshooting:

Adjust Tension: Ensure your tension is consistent throughout. Practice pulling up loops evenly.

Use Correct Hook Size: Make sure you are using the appropriate hook size for both the large loops and the smaller working stitches.

Relax: If you are holding the yarn or broomstick too tightly, try to relax your grip to create more consistent loops.

Uneven Edges

Issue: Your project might have uneven edges or a wavy appearance.

Troubleshooting:

Check Foundation Chain: Ensure the foundation chain is not too tight. It should be loose enough to allow the loops to sit comfortably.

Consistent Loop Size: Make sure each loop is the same size to prevent uneven edges.

Block Your Work: Blocking can help even out the edges and set the shape of your project.

Gaps Between Stitches

Issue: Large gaps or holes might appear between the loops or stitches.

Troubleshooting:

Check Loop Placement: Ensure that loops are placed closely together and that they are not too spread out.

Correct Tension: Maintain consistent tension to avoid gaps between stitches.

Review Stitch Pattern: Verify that your stitch pattern is being followed correctly, especially when changing colors or stitches.

Difficulty Removing Broomstick

Issue: The broomstick might be stuck or difficult to remove.

Troubleshooting:

Check Loop Size: If loops are too tight, try to loosen them slightly before removing the broomstick.

Use a Smooth Tool: Ensure that your broomstick or knitting needle is smooth and free of any rough spots that might catch the yarn.

Practice: If you're new to Broomstick Lace, practicing the technique will help you become more comfortable with removing the broomstick smoothly.

Stitch Count Off

Issue: The stitch count might be incorrect, leading to uneven rows or misaligned patterns.

Troubleshooting:

Count Regularly: Regularly count your stitches and loops to ensure you are on track with the pattern.

Mark Rows: Use stitch markers to keep track of pattern repeats and rows.

Recount Before Working: If you notice an issue, recount your stitches and loops to identify where the mistake occurred.

Project Doesn't Lay Flat

Issue: The finished project may curl or not lay flat.

Troubleshooting:

Block Your Project: Blocking can help shape and flatten your project. Wet or steam block to even out the edges and smooth the fabric.

Check Pattern Accuracy: Ensure that the pattern was followed correctly, as some patterns might require specific techniques to lay flat.

General Tips

Choose the Right Yarn and Hook

Yarn: Opt for yarns with good drape and smooth texture. Cotton or acrylic yarns are popular choices. Avoid yarns that are too fuzzy or have a lot of texture, as they can make it difficult to see and manage the loops.

Hook: Use a large hook or broomstick handle for creating loops and a smaller hook for working stitches. Ensure both tools are smooth to prevent snagging.

Maintain Consistent Tension

Loops: Keep your loops consistent in size. Too-tight loops can make them difficult to work with, while too-loose loops can lead to an uneven fabric.

Practice: Practice pulling up loops with consistent tension to improve your control and uniformity.

Start with Simple Projects

Beginner Projects: Start with smaller, simpler projects like dishcloths or coasters to get comfortable with the Broomstick Lace technique before moving on to more complex items.

Patterns: Choose beginner-friendly patterns that allow you to focus on mastering the basics without adding extra complications.

Use Stitch Markers

Track Progress: Use stitch markers to keep track of rows, pattern repeats, or where color changes occur. This helps ensure accuracy and consistency.

Placement: Place markers at the beginning of each row or where specific pattern changes occur.

Practice Blocking

Blocking: Blocking helps shape and set your project, making the finished piece look more polished and professional. Wet or steam block your work according to the yarn's care instructions.

Shaping: Use blocking to correct any irregularities or curling edges.

Be Patient with Loop Removal

Removal: Removing the broomstick can be tricky. Take your time and be gentle to avoid stretching or distorting the loops.

Practice: If you're new to the technique, practice removing the broomstick until you become more comfortable and efficient.

Read and Follow Patterns Carefully

Pattern Instructions: Follow pattern instructions closely to avoid mistakes. Pay attention to details such as loop counts, stitch types, and pattern repeats.

Understand Abbreviations: Familiarize yourself with common crochet abbreviations and terminology used in patterns.

Experiment with Different Patterns

Variety: Explore different stitch patterns and techniques to add variety and creativity to your projects. Combining Broomstick Lace with other crochet stitches can create unique designs.

Design Your Own: Once you're comfortable with the basics, experiment with designing your own patterns or modifying existing ones.

Keep Your Workspace Organized

Tools and Yarn: Keep your crochet tools and yarn organized to make your crafting experience more enjoyable and efficient.

Lighting: Ensure you have good lighting to clearly see your stitches and loops, which is especially important for detailed work.

Have Fun and Experiment

Enjoy the Process: Crochet should be enjoyable. Experiment with different yarns, patterns, and techniques to find what you love.

Learn Continuously: Don't be afraid to make mistakes and learn from them. Each project is an opportunity to improve your skills.

CONCLUSION

Broomstick Lace Crochet is a unique and versatile technique that combines the elegance of lacework with the versatility of crochet. By using a broomstick handle or large knitting needle to create loops, you can produce intricate and airy patterns suitable for a wide range of projects, from delicate shawls and vests to cozy blankets and stylish accessories.

Starting with simple projects helps beginners master the basics of loop creation and stitch work. As you gain confidence, you can progress to more complex patterns and incorporate advanced techniques like color gradients, lace panels, and intricate motifs. Troubleshooting common issues such as inconsistent loop sizes, uneven edges, or gaps will improve your craftsmanship and ensure a polished finish.

With practice and patience, Broomstick Lace Crochet allows you to create beautiful and functional items that showcase your creativity and skill. Enjoy experimenting with different yarns, patterns, and designs, and let your imagination guide you in crafting stunning crochet pieces.